C is for Cat.

D is for Depression.

Published by Scholastic India Pvt. Ltd.
A subsidiary of Scholastic Inc., New York, 10012 (USA).
Publishers since 1920, with international operations in Canada, Australia, New Zealand, the United Kingdom, India, and Hong Kong.

For information regarding permission, write to:
Scholastic India Pvt. Ltd.
A-27, Ground Floor, Sigma Centre
Infocity-1, Sector 34, Gurgaon-122001 (India)

First edition: September 2020
This reprint edition: February 2026

ISBN-13: 978-93-9018-911-3

Printed at Saurabh Printers Pvt.Ltd.

C is for Cat. D is for Depression.

KAIRAVI BHARAT RAM

Illustrations by
Priya Kuriyan

SCHOLASTIC
New York Toronto London Auckland
Sydney New Delhi Hong Kong

A MESSAGE FROM SCHOLASTIC INDIA

Dear Reader,

The book you hold in your hand is very special indeed. The world is constantly changing and can be a difficult, and sometimes, perilous place to navigate. And through all the ups and downs we experience, taking care of our mental well-being is crucial for us to give our best.

This beautiful book has been put together with a lot of love and care. I hope that you like this unique true story.

And remember, you're never alone.

Shantanu Duttagupta
Publisher

Author's Note

You probably picked up this book out of curiosity, or because someone has asked you to read it or maybe because you feel like you can relate to it. No matter what the reason is, I'm proud of you! It takes a strong person to hit pause on real life in order to dive into learning something new.

Think of this as a story. A story of a girl who represents us all, and of her journey as she goes through the darkest of times to finally come out into the light. I want you to hold this girl in your mind as a symbol–that in the end, 'It'll all be okay'.

So don't hesitate to cry and laugh along with her, and in her, find a friend who can support you or help you support someone important through all the challenges that may come their way.

Because you're never too old or too young to make a difference, whether it is in someone else's life or even in your own.

Love,
Kairu

Today, I'm going to talk about something I've felt for a long time,

In case, maybe, just maybe, you share these thoughts of mine.

As kids we are taught all the important things we need to know,
The periodic table, the constellations, the world maps they do show.

They tell us: A is for apple and B is for ball,
That C is for cat and D is for doll.

But that's not all. From kids, why do we hide,

That for another word, D can also be applied?

Depression. There I said it. It's always spoken of with a hush.
Such an important topic upon which in school they don't even brush.

You may have heard the word but not know what it means,
It's hard to really understand unless in depression you have been.

It's not just a phrase used to describe when you're upset.
It's a proper condition that sometimes some people get.

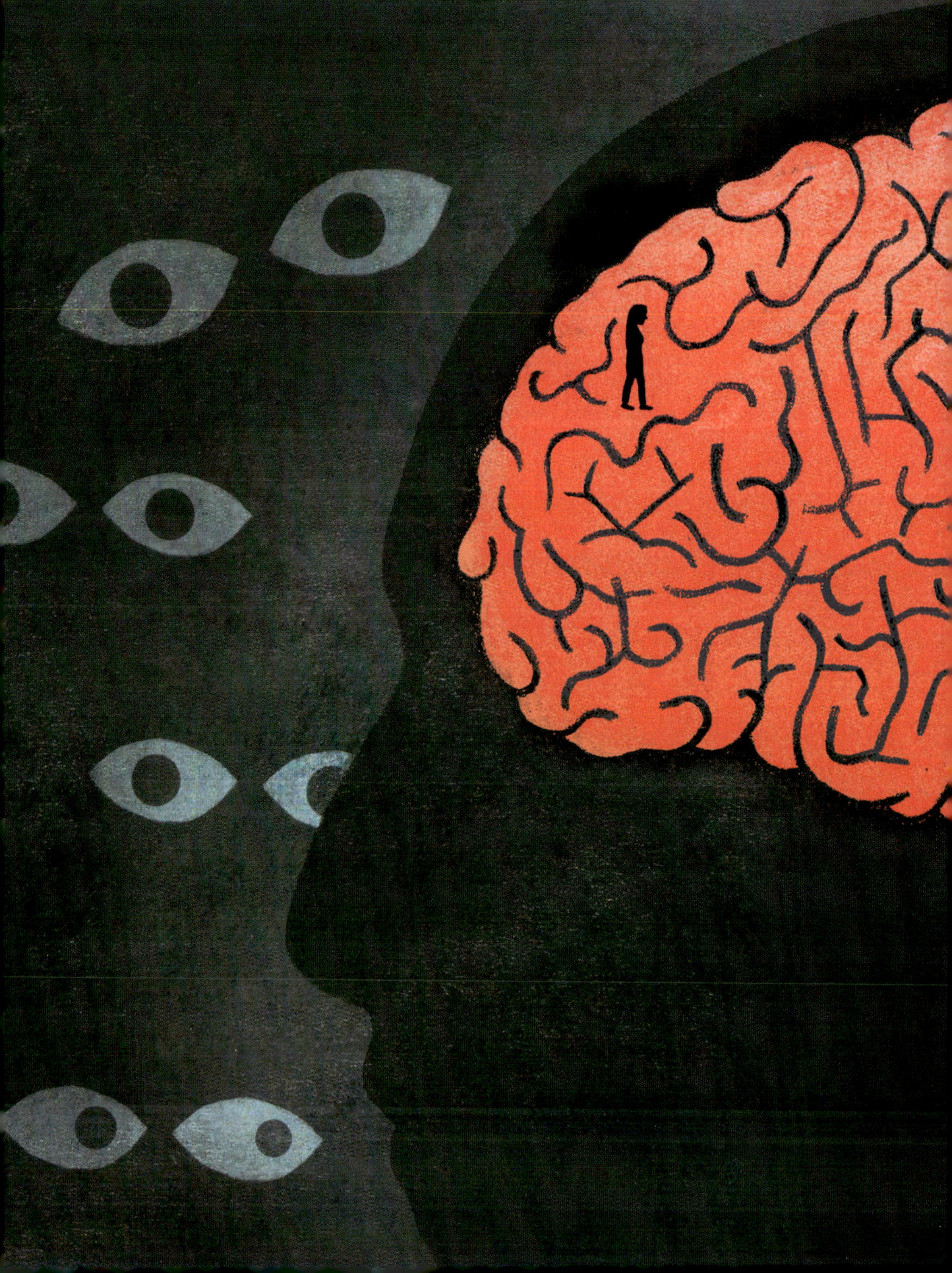

Because of events around them or because maybe,
Their bodies and minds are out of sync chemically.

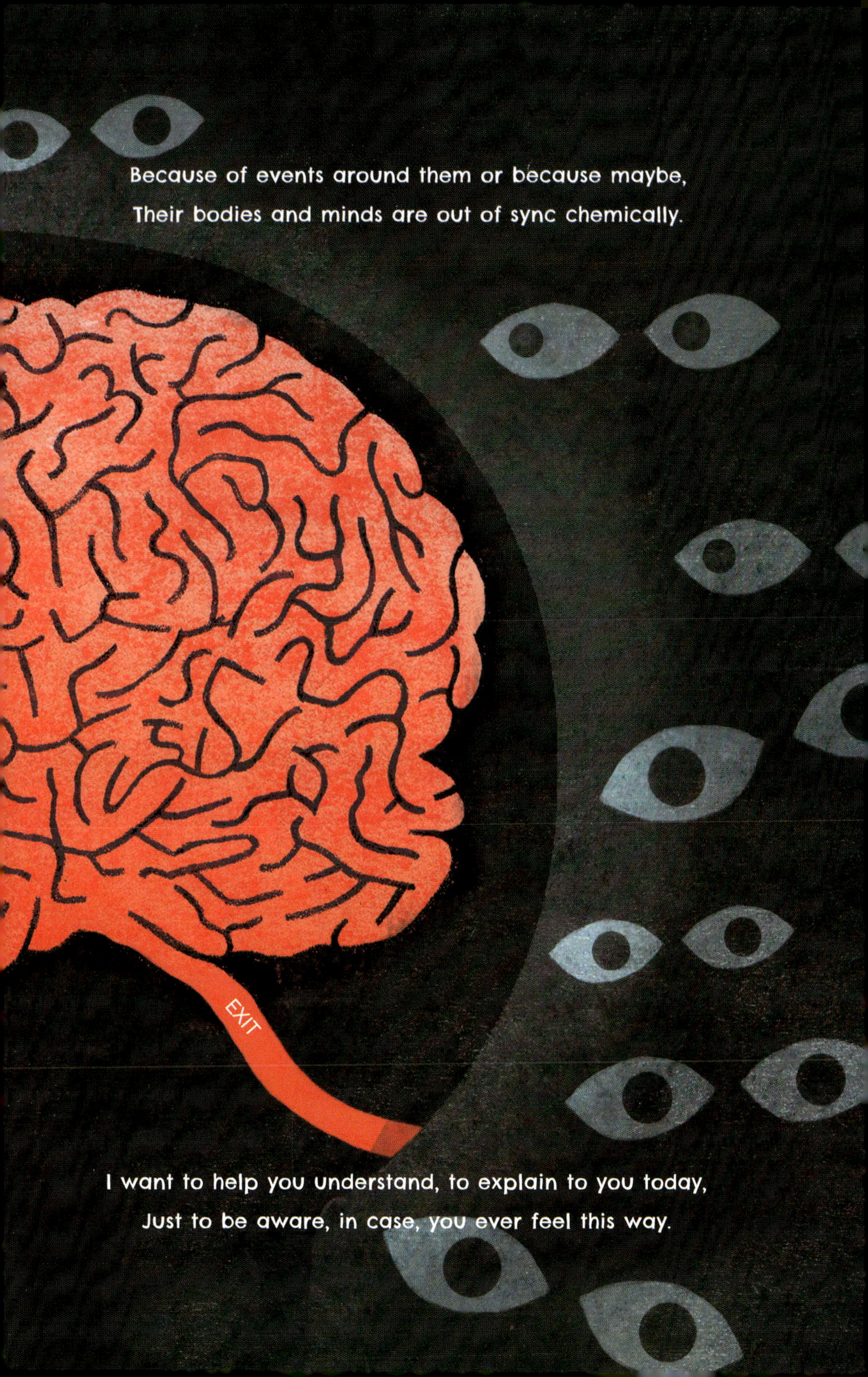

I want to help you understand, to explain to you today,
Just to be aware, in case, you ever feel this way.

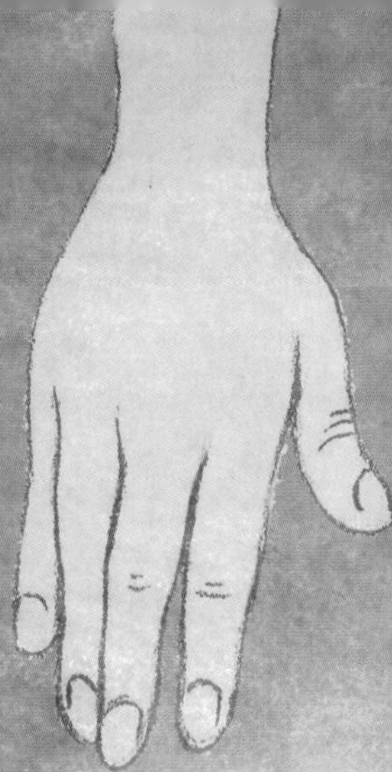

Or if someone around you is going through this,
And their world is falling apart and their mind is in crisis,

Then you can lean forward and offer a helping hand.
'Cause you have read about depression, and now you understand.

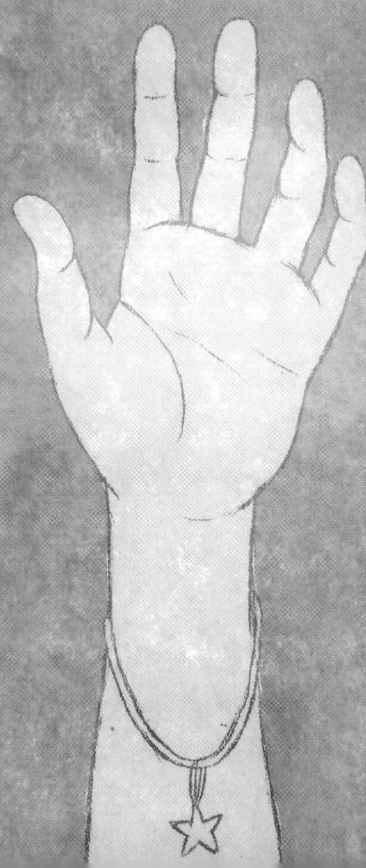

One day things are fine; you're happy and carefree.
Suddenly, the switch flips and in comes negativity.

It's almost like a movie, full of colour and so bright,
That loses all vibrancy and is now black and white.

Or like walking around with a dark cloud over your head,
Around you it's sunny, but on you there's a storm instead.

That storm represents the turmoil in your brain,
The gloomy atmosphere created by thunder and rain.

Another way to describe it is, it's like falling down a hole,
Falling head first, spinning out of control.

How deep is the hole? I've been falling for so long.
Shouldn't this stop at some point? It just feels so wrong.

The further you go, the more you believe,

That this dark hole, you'll never ever leave.

Or it feels like there's a radio going on in your head,
Spouting negative commentary about everything being said.

When you try to talk to someone, it says you're boring, no fun.
When you try and step out of your room, it says: go back, run.

Or when you have dreams and aspirations, it says you can't.
'You don't deserve it' is going on in your head like a chant.

But here's my favourite description: it's like drowning in the sea.
Everyone around you can swim but nope, not me.

Fighting the currents, getting exhausted day by day,
How can I stop this? Is there any way?

Or you're surrounded by four walls closing in on you,
It's getting smaller and smaller, there's nothing you can do.

It's like a bad dream, you're really out of luck,
And every night thereafter, in the same dream you're stuck.

But even after a nightmare, you wake up, you're okay.
But this just doesn't stop, it happens every day.

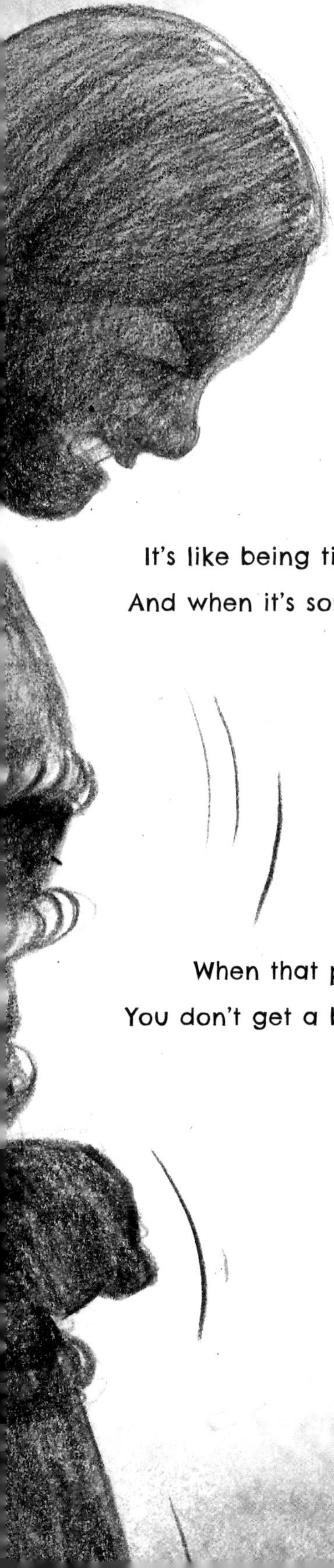

It's like being tied to someone with an invisible rope.
And when it's someone you hate, it's very hard to cope.

When that person is you, it's even more hard,
You don't get a break; you're just getting more scarred.

It's like getting a fever and feeling very sick,
But it's more than just a flu, on your mind it plays a trick.

It makes you believe you deserve this, this is your fate,
Stuck with this sickness forever, stuck in this state.

It mimics that feeling of being away on an unpleasant trip,
And wanting to go home so badly, you feel you're going to flip.

Except you are home, in your room, the only place you know.

But you are still uneasy; where do you desire to go?

It's like being in a tunnel but there's no light at the end.
You realize, in here, your whole life you will spend.

Not only that, there's sticky mud sucking at your feet,
Making it hard to move forward, making you accept defeat.

Or like you're on an endless journey with rocks on your back,
And the negativity in your mind is on the mode to attack.

And because you're bent down low, all you can see is the ground,
Making you feel hopeless, even though good things are around.

But hope is a funny thing, either it's in you or it's not,
It's one of those things that even in the best school can't be taught.

So when you are low, and hope is out of the door,
I have a solution for you that will work for sure.

Close your eyes and think of the people you hold dear,
Then even the worst thoughts will slowly start to disappear.

Seeing you suffer, remember your mom's tear-filled eyes,
Remember the hours your dad sat with you giving you advice.

Take things step by step, enjoy life's little joys,
Like a sleepover with the girls, or a game of catch with the boys.

There is a solution for everything you feel,
These thoughts are just in your mind though they feel totally real.

Because if you're drowning, you can
learn how to float,
Or someone will rescue you in their little boat.

Or if you're falling, you'll eventually hit the floor,
And from there the only way is up, that's for sure.

If it's a nightmare, one day, the alarm will ring,
It'll just be a bad memory, a past thing.

And the tunnel that looked like it had no light at the end,
Has happiness awaiting you at the very next bend.

And that unwanted friend who annoyed you all day,
You guys now get along; you don't mind that she'll stay.

'Cause you may never be 'normal', like the next guy in line,

But is anyone really normal? Is anyone really fine?

Depression may be like a dog that's around you always,
But you've trained him well. He now listens, sits and stays.

And if you ever need motivation, you can think about me.

I'm now finally able to separate depression from reality.

And I'll never regret this journey that I have been on,
It gives me something to be proud of, something to reflect upon.

And I promise things will change like they did for me.
One day from this darkness, you'll finally be free.

Facing it head-on is best, you've got nothing to fear,

After all I've been through, I'm still HERE.

Acknowledgements

I'm usually not one for lengthy acknowledgements but if any book ever deserved a string of 'thank yous', it's this one. Because this isn't just gratitude towards people who made the book possible but also to the people who brought me across the finish line, saved me from drowning and loved me till I could love myself.

Mumma, Papa, Apoo and, of course, Google. I'm going to say the most clichéd line but you really are the best family in the world. None of us are perfect, but the way you learnt, adjusted and moulded yourself to become exactly what I needed is something I can never thank you enough for.

My Dadu, my first best friend. Hands on and fully involved even in this journey, just like you have been in every part of my life.

My House No. 1 family. Thatha, Thathi and, of course, Maahir and Ahaana for unknowingly inspiring me to write this book.

My real-life guardian angels, Ananya and Mausi. This book is born from the thousands of hours we've spent talking and crying and understanding. This book is here because of you, and today, I am here because of you.

Yuvi bhaiya, thank you for being my partner in absolutely everything and for proving to me that I was worth it by loving and caring for me the way you do.

Meher, Srivats, Ash, Sammy, Neha, Sara, Nakita, Vedu, Vinayak and Adi. My little army of soldiers, who bravely fought all my demons when I couldn't.

The Scholastic team and Shantanu Duttagupta, for being such a safe space and for humouring all my crazy ideas, and for making my craziest one of all into this beautiful book.

Priya Kuriyan, for being my partner in this journey and breathing life into my words. You read my mind and portrayed it in a way that was far beyond anything I could have imagined.

And lastly, Dr Shelja, you wrote about me in your book and I think it's my turn to return the favour. I am at a loss for words, and you know that doesn't happen often. How do you say thank you to someone who's saved you from your darkest moments and made you who you are today? So I'll just say, thank you for being way more than my doctor, thank you for being my friend.

To all of you above, we did it! We made it to the other side and now maybe our little journey will help other little girls and boys who need someone to tell them, 'It'll all be okay', just like you did for me!

ABOUT THE AUTHOR

Kairavi Bharat Ram graduated from The Shri Ram School in 2016. She is currently studying Fashion Management at London College of Fashion. She is also a make-up blogger on Instagram under the name @blushmasterk. She has co-authored two books on mythology as well–*Ramayana in Rhyme* and *Krishna in Rhyme*. She is an advocate for mental health having suffered from depression for many years. In her free time, she likes to watch Korean dramas, write poems, cuddle her dog Google and dream about starting her own make-up line.

ABOUT THE ILLUSTRATOR

Priya Kuriyan is a children's book writer-illustrator, comics maker and chronic doodler. She has directed educational films for the Sesame street show (India) and the Children's Film Society of India (CFSI) and has illustrated numerous children's books for various Indian publishers. She lives and works in the city of Bangalore and in her spare time makes funny caricatures of its residents.

OTHER BOOKS BY KAIRAVI BHARAT RAM

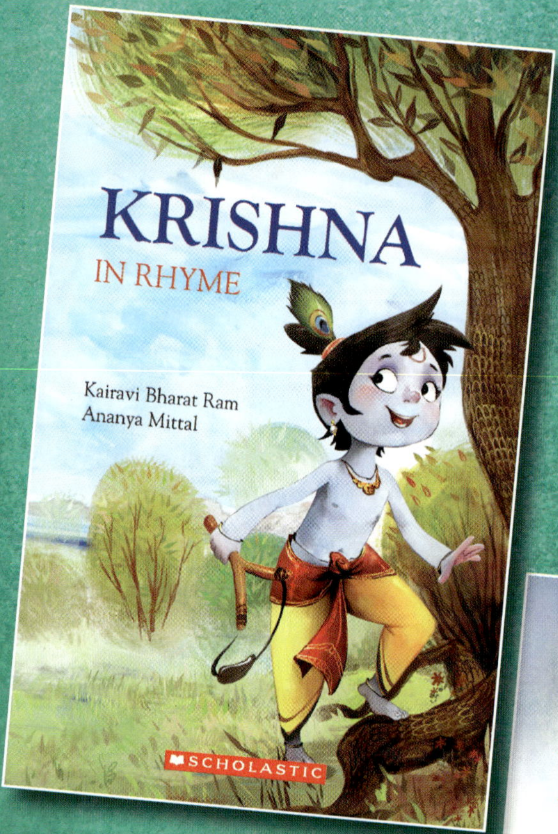

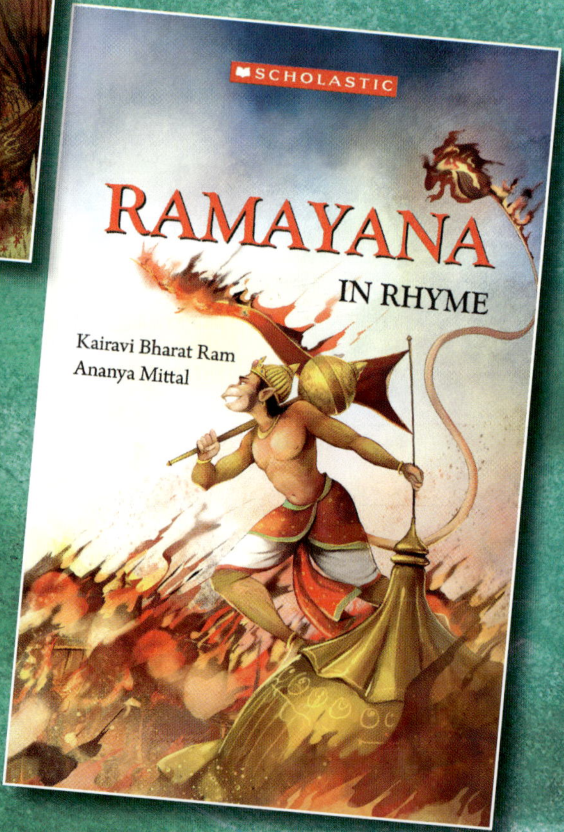

OTHER BOOKS BY PRIYA KURIYAN